concession stand

commercial

dance

rudder

bargain

musician

baggage

twist

jigsaw

fizz

rhythm

salmon

art gallery

atlas

fiance

tearful

cockpit

telephone booth

dead end

taxes

professor

vanish

cell phone charger

stage

bulldog

economics

dodgeball

fog

servant

nanny

raft

pharaoh

cheat

downpour

time machine

dizzy

pain

ticket

coworker

elope

injury

jaw

dawn

chess

swamp

biscuit

cattle

carnival

firefighter

dress shirt